Tarantula's big plan

by Clint Twist

First published in Great Britain in 2006 by ticktock Media Ltd.,
Unit 2, Orchard Business Centre, North Farm Road, Tunbridge Wells, Kent, TN2 3XF
ISBN 1 86007842 7 PB Printed in China
A CIP catalogue record for this book is available from the British Library.

Picture Credits
Alamy: 8 (Danita Delimont), 15t (David Haynes), 17b (Jonathan Plant). Getty Images: 6-7 (Digital Vision). FLPA: 2-3 (Mark Jones/Minden Pictures), 4-5 (Michael & Patricia Fogden/Minden Pictures), 5 side panel, 9t, 12, 18, 19 side panel, 24b (Mark Moffett/Minden Pictures), 7t (Chris Mattison), 22 (Claus Meyer/Minden Pictures). OSF: 5, 13b (Nick Gordon), 21 side panel, 27t (Densey Clyne Productions). Science Photo Library: 9 side panel, 13 side panel (Steve Gschmeissner), 11 side panel, 17 side panel, (Sinclair Stammers), 15 side panel (Scott Camazine), 23 side panel (Andrew Syred).
We would be pleased to insert the appropriate acknowledgements in any subsequent edition of this publication.

CONTENTS

What are Tarantulas?

Tarantulas are spiders. Spiders are wingless, eight-legged, minibeasts. They are not insects, because insects have only six legs. Tarantulas are the largest of all spiders and the distance between their outstretched legs can be as much as 30 cm.

How do tarantulas live?

Like all spiders, tarantulas are predators. They are carnivores (meat-eaters) that hunt and kill other animals. Spiders mainly eat insects and other minibeasts but tarantulas sometimes hunt much bigger prey, such as birds.

Understanding minibeasts

Spiders belong to a group of minibeasts known as arachnids. Other kinds of arachnid are scorpions, ticks, and mites. Arachnids, like insects, are part of a larger group of minibeasts known as arthropods. Adult arthropods do not have an inner skeleton made of bones like we do. Instead, they have a tough outer skin called an exoskeleton.

Tarantulas prefer to live in hot, tropical regions like this one in Venezuela, South America.

Tarantulas, like this red-kneed tarantula in Costa Rica, are a big type of spider.

Where do tarantulas live?

Spiders are able to live anywhere except the North and South poles (where it is too cold), and on the tops of the highest mountains. Tarantulas like to live in warm places like deserts and rainforests.

Spiders, such as this tarantula, have to shed their exoskeleton in order to grow.

A large tarantula has a body that is about 5 cm across with eight legs. Each leg can measure up to 10 cm in length. Most tarantulas are covered in lots of hairs.

All spiders have two parts to their body: the prosoma and the abdomen. The front part of the prosoma is the spider's head and has eyes, a brain, strong jaws and sharp fangs.

legs

Toward the back of the prosoma is a pair of short pedipalps (arms) that are used for holding food close to their jaws. Behind the pedipalps, there are four pairs of walking legs.

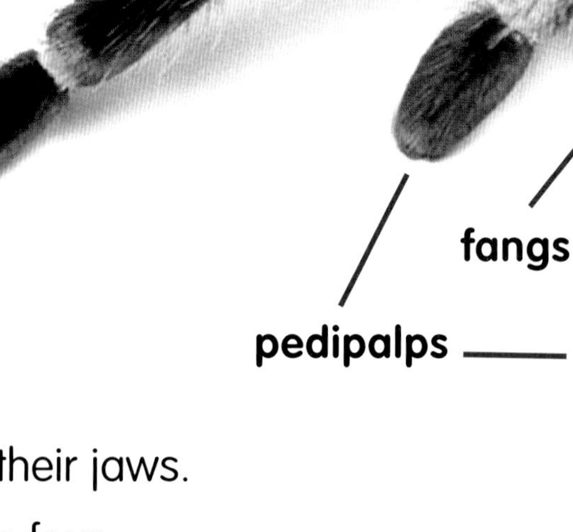

Spider shape

The earliest spiders probably had three parts to their bodies: head, thorax and abdomen, just like insects. With spiders, the head and thorax gradually joined together into a single part, called the prosoma. With insects, however, the head and the thorax stayed separate.

The narrowest part of a spider's body is in between the prosoma and the abdomen as shown here on this red-rumped tarantula.

abdomen

prosoma

A Mexican red-kneed tarantula.

Inside the abdomen are special parts that are used to produce silk. Tarantulas use silk to catch their prey and to line their nests.

There are two main parts to a spider's body - the prosoma and the abdomen, such as in this Brazilian pink tarantula.

Home Snug Home

Tarantulas live long lives. They live by themselves and do not form family groups. Females can live to be more than 35 years old, while males live to only about half that age.

They like to live in safe, dry, permanent nests. A tarantula may live in the same nest for the whole of its adult life.

Some tarantulas like to live in holes in trees, but most prefer to live underground like this one in Panama.

A tarantula digs its own burrow, which can extend as far as 75 cm below the ground. Using its strong jaws, it can easily cut through even the hardest, sun-baked soil.

Tarantulas, such as this one in North Arizona, USA, keep the opening to their burrow small to stop other creatures getting in.

The opening of the burrow is kept as small as possible. There is usually only one place in the burrow where there is enough room for the tarantula to turn around.

This metallic pink toe tarantula has spun a silk lining to make its burrow nice and snug.

Silk production

Insects and spiders can both produce silk. With insects, it is the larvae (young) that produce silk. They spin a protective cocoon of silk around their soft bodies while growing. With spiders, however, it is the adults that spin silk. Some types of spiders use silk for building webs, and some spiders use silk for making trip lines and to line their nests.

A tarantula's prey wrapped in silk.

Trip Lines

Most tarantulas spend most of their long lives hiding in their burrows and waiting for their prey to come along. After a big meal, a tarantula does not need to eat again for several weeks.

Some spiders spin webs to catch flying insects, or to trap insects that crawl along the ground, but tarantulas do not. Although they do not spin webs, tarantulas do use their silk for catching prey.

If possible, a tarantula will spin a series of trip lines that spread out from its burrow like the spokes of a wheel.

Tarantulas do not spin webs in order to catch their prey. They attack prey with their fangs just like this raft spider.

The tarantula settles down in its nest and waits for a minibeast or other animal to stumble into the trip line.

One end of the line is attached to something solid, while the other end is attached to the tarantula's silken nest lining. Sitting in its nest, the tarantula can feel when its prey touches the line.

When it feels a tug on the line, a tarantula (like this Antilles pink toe) dashes out to kill its prey.

Paralysing poison

All spiders are equipped with venom, which is produced by special glands in the head and is injected into the victim through sharp, hollow fangs in the spider's jaw. The purpose of the venom is to paralyse victims so that they cannot move. Spiders prefer their prey to be still alive when they start eating.

Tarantulas are all carnivores (meat-eaters). This one is eating a grasshopper in Ecuador.

Prowling for Prey

Some tarantulas do not like waiting for their prey, so they regularly go out and hunt. These include the largest, bird-eating tarantulas.

By day, it is dangerous for tarantulas to go out of their burrows. Their large size makes them a tempting target for any spider-eating birds that may be flying above them.

By night it is much safer – although not completely safe, so there is less chance of the predator (the spider) becoming the prey.

Daytime can be a dangerous time for tarantulas, as they may be attacked by predators.

Tarantulas live mainly on a diet of large insects. The biggest tarantulas are able to attack small mammals, lizards, and even birds that are sitting on nests.

Larger tarantulas can eat things as big as birds.

If a tarantula cannot find any large prey, it will collect lots of small insects. The spider will wrap them together with strands of silk and then eat them all at the same time.

A goliath birdeating tarantula eating a snake in Venezuela.

Liquid steel

Spider silk starts out as a liquid produced by special glands inside the abdomen. The liquid is squirted out of the spider's body by tiny nozzles at the base of the abdomen that are called spinnerets. The spider uses its legs to pull out the strands of liquid silk until they harden but remain sticky. Spider silk is much stronger than steel wire of the same thickness.

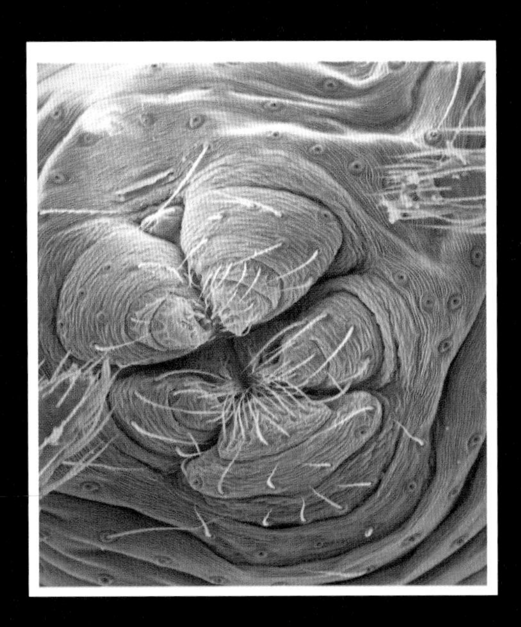

A tarantula's spinnerets; where its silk comes out.

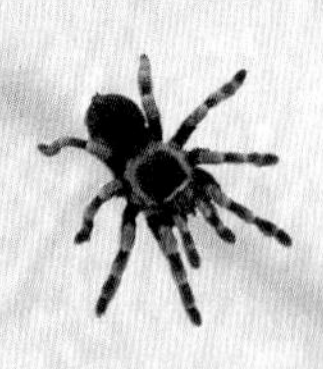

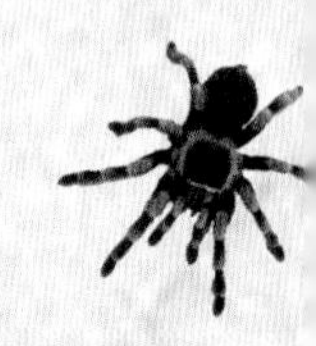

Spider Senses

Some spiders have excellent eyesight; while others, including tarantulas, have very bad eyesight. All spiders, however, can feel vibrations, and this is how they get information about their surroundings.

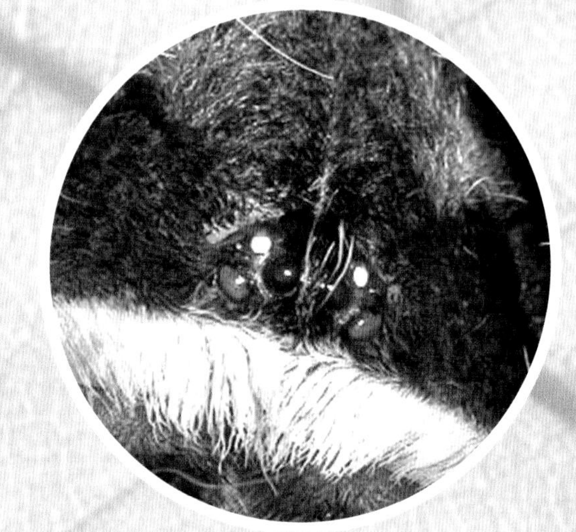

Most tarantulas' eyesight is very bad.

Tarantulas can feel the tiny vibrations moving through each of their eight legs. Because their legs are spread out, they can also tell where the vibrations are coming from.

All spiders have hairs for feeling vibration. Even spiders that do not look hairy have these hairs.

Tarantulas' hairs can pick up tiny vibrations.

Tarantulas have eight small eyes at the front of the prosoma. Each eye can do little more than tell the difference between light and darkness. All together they are just enough for the tarantula to be able to see movement.

Tarantulas use their hairy legs to find out about their surroundings, like this red kneed tarantula from Mexico.

Paired eyes

Most spiders have eight eyes. Some have six or four, and some have only two. Usually, but not always, the eyes are arranged in two rows. Some spiders, such as jumping spiders, have two hunting eyes that can produce clear images. Most spiders, however, are like the tarantula, and have to make do with bad eyesight.

Spiders' eyes always come in pairs. This is a jumping spider, which has four eyes.

Massive Jaws

There are two main groups of spiders according to which way their jaws work: Tarantulas belong to the group that has jaws that strike downwards.

A tarantula's fangs are on the front of the prosoma.

Tarantulas have two sharp fangs that they can bring down either together, or again and again one after the other until their victims stop moving.

These fangs are designed like a pair pincers.

The other group of spiders have jaws designed to strike inwards. The fangs can be brought together so that the fangs meet like a pair of pincers. These fangs are better than the downward striking jaws because they stop the victim getting away.

The fangs of this Chile rose tarantula are large and sharp enough to pierce even the toughest insect exoskeleton.

Liquefied food

Spiders do not chew and crunch their food – they just slurp it up. Once the prey stops moving, the spider dribbles digestive juices into the wound made by its jaws. These juices turn the prey's insides into semi-liquid goo that the spider sucks and slurps into its mouth.
After a spider has finished eating, all that is left is a scatter of tiny, dried up pieces that the spider cannot eat.

A crab spider sinking its fangs into a honey bee.

Search for a Mate

Tarantulas develop very slowly and they are not able to mate until they are about 10 years old. Mating normally takes place during the hottest and driest part of the year.

Males and female tarantulas live separately, but they do not use any way of communicating over long distances to find each other. Instead, finding a mate is a matter of going out and hoping that you bump into one.

A female California tarantula is alerted to a male outside her nest by her trip lines.

A Brazilian salmon birdeating tarantula defending itself.

Mating can be a risky business for males because female tarantulas usually prefer eating to mating – and they are quite happy to eat male tarantulas.

The male has to lift the female up in order to mate, just like this pampas gold tarantula is doing.

When a male is lucky enough to bump into a willing female, it does not mean he will get home safely. After mating, the female may still decide that the male will make a tasty snack!

Safety sound

Spiders can make sound in a number of ways, such as by rubbing their legs together or drumming their legs on the ground. Many spiders use these sounds for simple communication. Males that are in search of a mate make a special safety sound when they are moving. If they make this sound they are less likely to be attacked and eaten by a female.

This jumping spider makes sure it is safe for him to mate with the female.

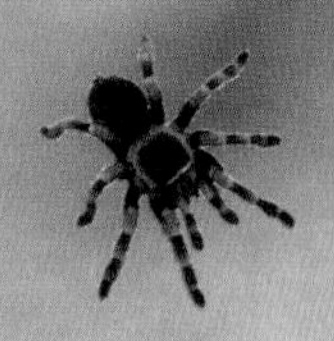

Spiderlings

Female tarantulas lay up to 1,000 eggs at a time. Each egg is very small and the female holds them together with strands of silk to make what is called an egg sac.

This ball-shaped mass of silk and eggs is about half the size of the female's body. The sticky silk prevents any of the eggs from being lost.

A female wolf spider carrying her egg sac.

The female usually just leaves the egg sac in the deepest part of her burrow, and does not give the eggs any special care. However, if it rains and the burrow floods, the female will carry the egg sac to safety.

The eggs hatch into tiny spiderlings that look just like miniature adults, except that they are very pale and almost colourless.

Tiny spiderlings hatch out of the egg sac.

The spiderlings can feed on tiny minibeasts in the soil that are much too small to fill up an adult tarantula.

Pet tarantulas can be born and raised in captivity.

Spider development

A spider's exoskeleton is not stretchy – it will not stretch as the spider grows in size. Instead, a growing spiderling develops a new, larger exoskeleton beneath the old, outgrown one. When the new exoskeleton is ready, the old one splits open and is discarded like a worn-out coat. This process is known as moulting.

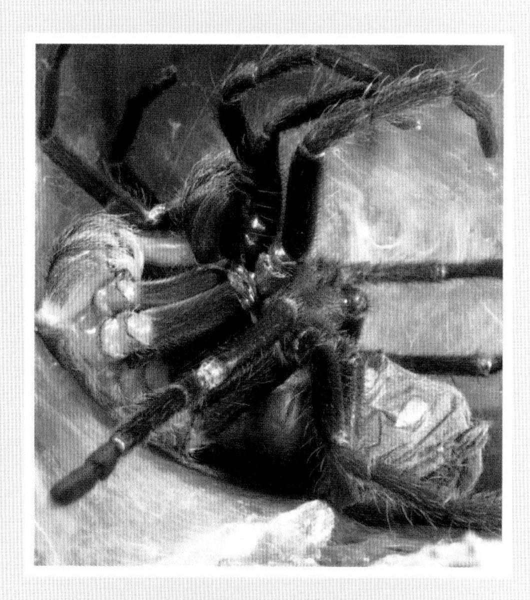

Tarantulas will have to moult several times before they are fully grown.

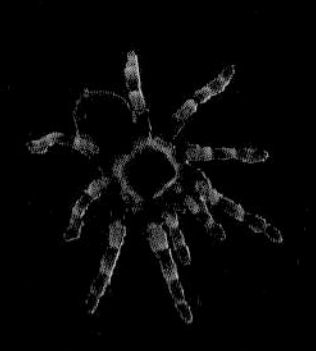

Tarantulas & Humans

The spiders that we call tarantulas, even the biggest bird-eating ones, are not really dangerous to human beings. Although the powerful jaws can deliver a painful bite, the venom of tarantulas is too weak to have much effect on human beings.

The name tarantula originally belonged to a much smaller, and supposedly much more dangerous spider.

This original tarantula is a European wolf spider (Lycosa tarentula). The wolf spider was first named tarantula after the town of Taranto in Southern Italy, where it lives.

The name Tarantula has now been given to the big hairy spiders, such as this birdeating tarantula.

A European wolf spider – the original tarantula.

Scientists long ago discovered that although this wolf spider gives a painful bite, it does not give humans any sort of disease. Because the original tarantula is actually a wolf spider, the name tarantula has since been given to the big hairy spiders.

Wolf spiders like this one are not as dangerous as people once thought.

Irritating Hairs

In addition to their sharp fangs and poisonous venom, tarantulas have other weapons hidden in their hairy covering. Some hairs are coated with poison and have sharp, fragile tips that easily break off. The poison on the hairs is not strong enough to harm a person, but if the tips become stuck in your skin they can cause a very irritating rash.

Tarantulas' hairs can cause an irritating rash on humans.

Other Spiders

There are more than 40,000 different species of spider. They all have two parts to their bodies and eight legs, but some spiders look very different to others.

Jumping spiders

This group is one of the largest of the spider groups. All jumping spiders have very good eyesight and they have two pairs of eyes. They jump on their prey (which can be up to 25 cm away) to catch it.

Jumping spiders have two pairs of eyes.

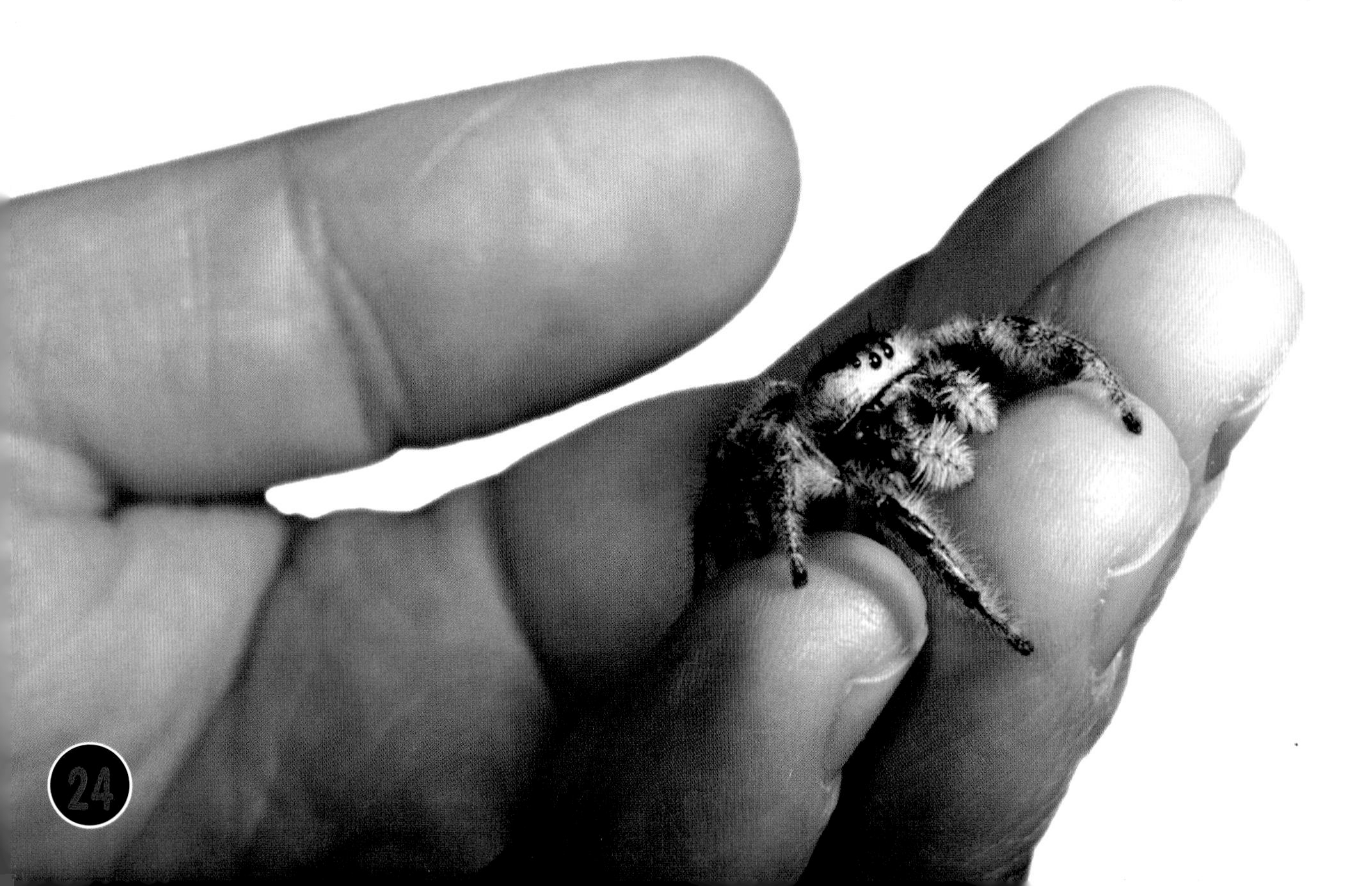

Curved spiny spider

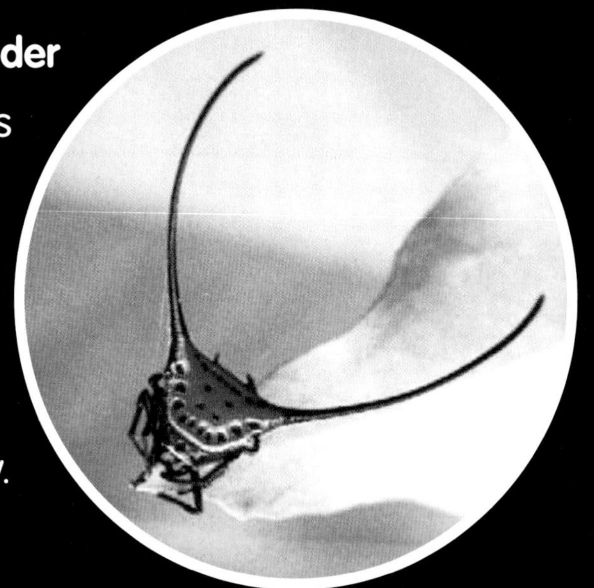

Some small spiders have spines and horns which give the spiders an unusual appearance. Scientists believe that the spiders developed these horns and spines because it makes them difficult for birds to swallow.

Flower spiders

These spiders are also called crab spiders because they often walk sideways the way crabs do. They have pale bodies and wait on flowers to catch visiting insects. Some flower spiders can change the colour of their bodies to match the flowers they are sitting on.

Black widow

Everyone should be able to recognize the famous black widow spider with its red marking. This small creature has fangs that deliver very poisonous venom. The bite of a black widow is very painful, and the venom is strong enough to kill children and old people.

Spider Behaviour

Many spiders live and hunt in much the same way as the tarantulas, but others have different ways of life – and very different ways of using their silk.

Web spinners

The most well-known spiders are those that spin webs between branches to catch flying insects. The spider sits at one corner of the web and waits for vibrations made by an insect tangled up in the web.

Net throwing spiders

These spiders do not bother spinning a big web fixed in one place. Instead they spin a small web like a piece of fishing net. The spider then holds this net between its two front pairs of legs and waits patiently on a branch. When an insect comes within reach, the spider drops its net to catch the victim.

Water spider

This spider is only found in fresh water. It spins a very dense web of silk, and then traps bubbles of air in the web. The air in the bubbles allows the spider to breathe underwater while it waits for prey such as tadpoles and baby fish.

Spitting spider

Spitting spiders have special venom-silk glands that allow them to spit two streams of poisonous silk. They attack their insect prey by covering their victims with a zigzag pattern of threads so they cannot fly away.

Find out More

Lifecycle

After mating with a male, the female produces an egg sac that can contains up to 1,000 tiny eggs. The egg sac is made of silk. Tiny spiderlings hatch from the eggs and emerge from the nest after a few weeks and have to find their own food. They grow into adults, who will then find a mate to make more eggs.

Fabulous Facts

Fact 1: Tarantulas can be as small as a fingernail to as big as a dinner plate.

Fact 2: For most people, tarantula bites are no worse than a bee sting.

Fact 3: Tarantulas have retractable claws, just like cats!

Fact 4: A tarantula spiderling will moult about 10 times before it becomes fully adult.

Fact 5: Fear of spiders is called Arachnophobia. It is one of the most common fears among humans.

Fact 6: Some tarantulas eat lizards, birds, even mice.

Fact 7: Tarantulas can be kept as a house pet in a terrarium.

Fact 8: On the average, female tarantulas live 20-30 years and males 10-12 years.

Fact 9: Tarantulas do not make webs to catch their prey. Instead, they hide and rush out to attack prey when it comes along.

Fact 10: There are more than 800 species of tarantulas.

Fact 11: When feeling threatened, some tarantulas make a loud hissing noise by rubbing the bristles on their legs together.

Fact 12: Some large animals and birds eat tarantulas. Some tarantula species are cannibalistic (they eat each other!).

Fact 13: Tarantulas like to live alone, and will attack other tarantulas that come near them uninvited.

Glossary

Abdomen – the largest part of a spider's body; the abdomen contains most of the important organs.

Arachnids – a group of minibeasts that includes spiders, scorpions, ticks, and mites.

Arachnophobia – the fear of spiders.

Arthropod – any minibeast that has jointed legs; insects and spiders are arthropods.

Cannibal – an animal that eats its own kind.

Carnivore – an animal that eats meat.

Cocoon – a protective covering of silk produced by insect larvae to protect their bodies while they transform into adults.

Exoskeleton – a hard outer covering that protects and supports the bodies of many minibeasts.

Fang – a long sharp tooth; some fangs are designed to inject venom.

Gland – a part of an animal's body that is used to make particular substances, e.g. silk.

Insect – a kind of mini-beast that has six legs, most insects also have wings.

Jaws – hinged structures around the mouth that allow some animals to bite and chew.

Larvae – grub-like creatures that are the juvenile (young) stage in the life cycle of many insects.

Lizard – one of a group of mainly small to medium-sized reptiles.

Mammal – one of a group of warm-blooded animals that have an internal skeleton and which feed their young on milk.

Minibeast – one of a large number of small land animals that do not have a skeleton.

Moulting – the shedding of a spider's exoskeleton, which they

need to do in order to grow.

Pedipalps – short, leg-like organs that a spider uses to hold its food.

Predator – an animal that hunts and eats other animals.

Prey – an animal that is eaten by other animals.

Prosoma – the front part of a spider's body that consists of the head and the thorax fused together into a single body part.

Retractable – Something that can be taken or drawn back.

Scorpion – a type of minibeast related to spiders, which has a long, flexible tail equipped with a venomous sting.

Silk – a natural thread produced by insect larvae and adult spiders.

Skeleton – an internal structure of bones that supports the bodies of large animals such as mammals, reptiles, and fish.

Spiderling – a young spider that is not yet fully grown.

Spinnerets – tiny nozzles on a spider's abdomen that are used to squirt out silk.

Tadpole – the juvenile (young) form of a frog or toad.

Terrarium – a container to keep plants and animals in.

Thorax – the middle part of an insect's body where the legs are attached.

Venom – a poison produced by an animal for use against other animals.

Web – network of silk threads produced by many spiders to catch flying insects.

index